Holy Places

The
Ganges

and other Hindu Holy Places

Victoria Parker

www.heinemann.co.uk/library
Visit our website to find out more information about **Heinemann Library** books.

To order:

☎ Phone 44 (0) 1865 888066

🗎 Send a fax to 44 (0) 1865 314091

💻 Visit the Heinemann Bookshop at www.heinemann.co.uk/library to browse our catalogue and order online.

First published in Great Britain by Heinemann Library, Halley Court, Jordan Hill, Oxford OX2 8EJ, a division of Reed Educational and Professional Publishing Ltd. Heinemann is a registered trademark of Reed Educational and Professional Publishing Ltd.

OXFORD MELBOURNE AUCKLAND JOHANNESBURG BLANTYRE
GABORONE IBADAN PORTSMOUTH NH (USA) CHICAGO

Designed by Joanna Sapwell and StoryBooks
Illustrations by Nick Hawken
Originated by Blenheim Colour
Printed by Wing King Tong, Hong Kong, China

ISBN 0 431 15511 9
06 05 04 03 02
10 9 8 7 6 5 4 3 2 1

British Library Cataloguing in Publication Data
Parker, Victoria
    The Ganges. – (Holy places)
    1.Rivers – religious aspects – Hinduism – Juvenile literature 2. Hindu pilgrims and pilgrimages – Juvenile literature 3. ganges river (India and bangladesh) – Juvenile literature
    I.title
    294.5'35'09541

Acknowledgements
The Publishers would like to thank the following for permission to reproduce photographs: Associated Press pp. 14, 22; Christine Osborne Pictures pp. 5, 15, 17, 18, 20; Circa Photo Library pp. 13, 16; Circa Photo Library/John Smith p. 11; Corbis p. 28; Images Of India Picture Agency pp. 7, 10, 19; Link Picture Library p.24; Trip/B Vikander p. 25; Trip/F Good pp. 21, 26; Trip/H Rogers pp. 8, 9, 12, 23, 27, 29.

Cover photograph reproduced with permission of Christine Osborne Pictures.

Our thanks to Anita Ganeri for her assistance in the preparation of this book.

Every effort has been made to contact copyright holders of any material reproduced in this book. Any omissions will be rectified in subsequent printings if notice is given to the Publisher.

Contents

What is the Ganges?   4

Who are the Hindus?   6

The Ganges legend   8

Why is Varanasi a holy city?   10

Shiva and the gods   12

What happens in a mandir?   14

Hindu worship at home   16

Pilgrimages to the Ganges   18

Hindu holy books   20

A Ganges festival   22

Other Hindu holy places   24

Hindu family ceremonies   26

Mahatma Gandhi – a Hindu holy man   28

Glossary   30

Index   32

Words printed in bold letters, **like this**, are explained in the Glossary on page 30.

What is the Ganges?

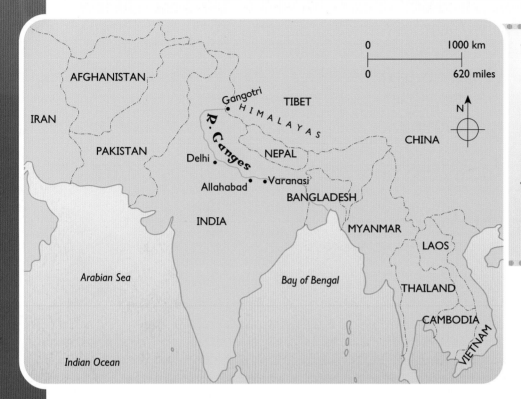

This map shows the River Ganges running through north India

India has several mighty rivers. One is the ancient River Ganges. The country of India is enormous. In some parts it is hot, dusty desert. In other parts, there are lush green plains. In the north is the snowy mountain range of the Himalayas. In the south are sandy beaches and ocean.

The Ganges begins almost 4000 metres (12,840 feet) high in the Himalayas. It flows from a **glacier** at a place called Gangotri. It flows down from here across the northern plains, through villages, towns and cities. After a journey of 2510 kilometres (1559 miles), the river finally reaches the coast and drains into the Indian Ocean at the Bay of Bengal.

Other faiths

Not all people who live in India are Hindus. There are several other religions. Two other important religions in India are Islam and **Sikhism**. Hindus and Sikhs share some of their holy places and festivals. There are also **Buddhists**, **Jains** and **Christians**.

Many of the people who live in India are Hindus. They follow a **religion** called Hinduism. There are seven great rivers in India that Hindus believe are **holy**. The holiest river of all is the Ganges. Every human, animal and plant on Earth needs water to live. Many people in India believe that a mighty river, which brings so much life wherever it flows, is a **symbol** of the power of God, who gives life to all things.

The River Ganges flows from an ice field high up in the Himalayas

Who are the Hindus?

The first great **civilization** in India grew up around the River Indus about 5000 years ago. 1500 years later, people called **Aryans** arrived to live there too. Over the next thousand years, each group's beliefs gradually mixed together to form the Hindu **religion**.

Most Hindus believe in a Supreme Spirit – who they call Brahman, and who is neither male nor female. They believe that everything is created by Brahman, and Brahman is in everything.

The spirit inside a person is their **soul**. Hindus believe that when a person dies, their soul moves on to a new life as another person, even an animal or plant. Being born again is called reincarnation. Through reincarnation, a soul lives many different lives.

All Hindus want to break free from the endless cycle of death and rebirth, so their soul can return to Brahman. Hindus say that this return to Brahman is a state of perfect happiness called **moksha**.

Because Hindus believe that a person's soul can be reborn as an animal, they treat all creatures kindly. Many Hindus do not eat meat.

Holy cows

Hindus have special respect for cows. They believe it is wrong to harm or kill a cow — even by accident. A person's soul is often pictured as a white cow. Cows are also givers of milk and so they are a **symbol** of the giver of life itself. Others think cows are special because in ancient times they were a form of wealth.

In India cows are allowed to wander wherever they like

The Ganges legend

Hindus honour the River Ganges as a goddess called Ganga. They believe that the Ganges is Ganga's home on Earth. They believe that in ancient times the Ganges did not flow on Earth. It began from the god Vishnu's toe and flowed through heaven. A story tells how the Ganges came down to Earth.

A king called Sagar once lost a precious horse and sent his sons to search for it. The princes accused a **holy** man of stealing it. The holy man was so angry that he wished them dead. The princes were burnt to ashes on the spot.

This painting shows the goddess Ganga pouring water onto the Earth

Gods and goddesses

Hindus believe that Brahman is so great that it is impossible to understand. Instead, they worship Brahman through many gods and goddesses. Each god or goddess represents a different power or aspect of Brahman.

The holy man announced that the princes' **souls** could only reach **moksha** if Ganga washed over the land. Neither King Sagar's grandson nor his son, Dilip, could bring Ganga down from heaven. Finally, Dilip's son, Bhagirath, offered many prayers that pleased Ganga and she began to flow towards Earth.

The rushing river was so mighty that she would have smashed the Earth to pieces, but the great god Shiva caught Ganga in his hair. He let her trickle down gently into the Himalayas. Bhagirath led Ganga to the sea, looking for the remains of the princes. As the holy waters washed over the ashes, the princes' souls were saved.

Many Hindu holy men live in lonely places to be on their own

Why is Varanasi a holy city?

These Hindus are bathing in the Ganges at Varanasi

The **holiest** place on the River Ganges is a city called Varanasi, also known as Benares. Hindus believe that the great god Shiva chose the city as his home on Earth. It has been a centre for Hindu teaching for thousands of years.

Many Hindus believe that Varanasi is the most **sacred** place to bathe in the waters of the Ganges. Every Hindu tries to go to Varanasi at least once in their lifetime, even if it means travelling thousands of miles to get there. Millions of Hindus visit the city every year. They go down broad steps called **ghats** to bathe in the holy river. Then they pray and worship at one of the many huge **temples** in the city.

DID YOU KNOW?

Another name for the city of Varanasi is Kashi. Kashi means 'to shine', so some people call Varanasi the city of light. Hindus believe that Varanasi is such a holy place, it is as if Brahman is shining brightly there, lighting up the way for souls to be saved.

Hindus also believe that Varanasi is the best place in which to die. When a Hindu dies, their body is cremated, or burnt. In Varanasi Hindu cremations happen at Manikamika ghat, which is also called the burning ghat. Hindus ask to be cremated here and to have their ashes scattered into the Ganges. They believe that if they do this their **souls** will be nearer to breaking out of the cycle of death and rebirth. Many Hindus who die in other places ask their relatives to bring their ashes to Varanasi to scatter them on the Ganges.

These cremations are taking place on Manikamika ghat

11

Shiva and the gods

The great god Shiva, who helped to bring the Ganges down to Earth, is one of three main Hindu gods. Brahma is the creator god, who makes everything in the universe. Vishnu is the protector god, who helps to keep a balance between good and evil. Shiva is the destroyer god, who wipes things out so that new things can be created.

Shiva's wife is a very important goddess. She is worshipped in different forms. As Parvati, she is gentle and kind. As Durga, she is a warrior who rides a lion and fights demons. As Kali, she is fierce and bloodthirsty, and helps people to overcome their fears.

This painting shows Ganisha, the elephant-headed god of wisdom

There are hundreds of other gods and goddesses who represent Brahman. Every Hindu has their own personal favourite, who they worship most of the time. Most Hindus have a **shrine** in their home with a picture or image of their favourite god in it. This **sacred** image of the god is called a **murti**.

This is a murti of Shiva dancing

13

What happens in a mandir?

Hindus worship at **temples** or mandirs. Each mandir is **dedicated** to a god, goddess or **holy** man. Each Hindu mandir has a priest to look after it.

When worshippers arrive, they take off their shoes, ring a bell and go inside to perform **puja**. Puja is a ceremony where Hindus show their love and respect for a god or goddess. The ceremony includes prayers and offerings to the god or goddess. The offering is usually some type of food. Any food that the worshipper offers is given back to them by the priest, with the god's blessing.

These Hindus are worshipping at a mandir at Varanasi

Sometimes the priest will lead the worshippers in an **arti** ceremony. This is when the priest lights five lamps in a steel tray and circles it in front of the **murti** while the worshippers **chant** a prayer. The priest sprinkles water over the worshippers to show that blessings from the god are coming down upon them. Then the arti tray is carried among the worshippers, to take the blessing of the temple god to them.

This is the town of Haridwar on the River Ganges

Hindu worship at home

This Hindu girl is worshipping before a shrine in her home

Hindus believe there are many different ways to worship. One is at home, making offerings of **puja** to a **murti** in a household **shrine**. There is no special day or time when Hindus are meant to perform puja. Most Hindus like to make offerings every morning and evening.

A Hindu family makes a shrine by putting a murti on a table or shelf, and decorating it with flowers, perfume and candles. If the family has a bottle of holy water from the River Ganges, they might put this before the murti too. There may also be pictures of other gods and goddesses, as well as the family's favourite.

Murtis of Shiva often show him dancing. Hindus believe that Shiva's energy keeps the universe changing and moving. Sometimes shrines to Shiva contain a carved stone column instead of a murti. This is called a **lingam**. It is Shiva's special **symbol**. There are a great number of them at Varanasi.

To perform puja, Hindus take off their shoes and stand or sit cross-legged before the murti. They set down little gifts of flowers or food as offerings. Then they concentrate by saying a verse of **holy** writing over and over again. This is called a **mantra**.

Often during puja, the mother of the family will look after the murti by carefully washing and drying it. Sometimes she will hang a garland of flowers or wrap a cloth robe around it. Hindus believe that by showing respect for the image of the god, they are showing respect for Brahman.

This mother is caring for a household murti

17

Pilgrimages to the Ganges

Hindus believe that if they do good deeds in this life, their next life will be closer to **moksha**. If they behave badly in this life, they will be reborn further away from moksha, perhaps as an animal. This idea is called **karma**. Hindus believe it is good karma if they make a journey to a **holy** place to worship there. This type of trip is called a **pilgrimage**.

There are many holy places along the Ganges besides Varanasi. Four are especially important. Gangotri is the **glacier** high in the Himalayas where the Ganges begins. Haridwar is where the Ganges flows down to the plains. Allahabad (also known as Prayag) is where the Ganges joins another holy river, the Yamuna. Sagara Island is where the Ganges flows into the sea.

Pilgrims bathing at the source of the River Ganges

Tirthas

Hindus believe that in holy places such as Varanasi, Ayodhya and Mathura (that all lie along the Ganges) a person can break free from Earth's cycle of death and rebirth and reach moksha. Such places are known as tirthas, which means crossing places. Hindus believe that it is easier to cross from this life into moksha at these places.

Once every twelve years, when the stars are in a special position in the sky, many Hindus make a pilgrimage to Allahabad. An enormous camp of tents springs up. Many pilgrims stay for a whole month to bathe in the waters and make offerings. This bathing fair is called Kumbh Mela. Over 10 million people attended the Kumbh Mela in 2001!

These Hindus are taking part in the Kumbh Mela at Allahabad

19

Hindu holy books

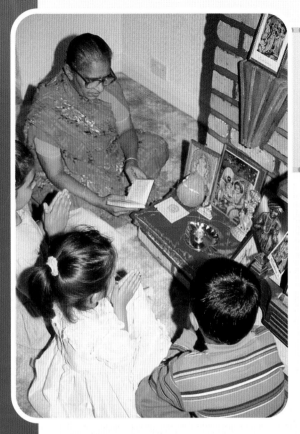

These children are praying with their grandmother at home

Hindus do not use the word Hinduism to describe their **religion**. They say that they follow Sanatan Dharma, which means 'eternal truths'. To Hindus Sanatan Dharma is not just a religion but a way of life.

The first Hindu teachings are over 3000 years old. They are known as the Vedas. Hindus believe they came from Brahman, the Supreme Spirit. The Vedas are beautiful poetry. They praise the gods of nature, such as the Sun, wind and fire.

Around 2500 years ago, wise men began to teach pupils about the Supreme Spirit and the **soul** in all things. Their teachings are now called the Upanishads.

Many ordinary people found it difficult to understand the Upanishads. To make it easier, the wise men made their teachings into stories about gods and goddesses. One **sacred** story called the *Mahabharata* is the longest poem in the world. Another long poem called the *Ramayana* tells many exciting tales about a prince called Rama. Rama was the great god Vishnu in a human form.

A temple and **ghats** in the town of Ayodhga on the River Ganges

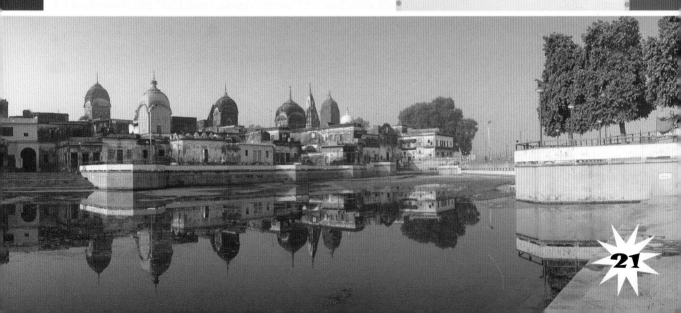

21

A Ganges festival

Hindus celebrate a festival called Navaratri, also known as Dassehra. Many believe this is the most important festival of all.

At Navaratri, Hindus worship Shiva's wife in the form of the goddess Durga. Durga is a fierce protector of good and destroyer of evil. Hindu **holy** books say she is the daughter of the mountain Himalaya.

This effigy of Durga is being lowered into the Ganges during the Dussehra festival

Hindus believe that each autumn, Durga comes to Earth for ten days to visit her family. Hindus show this by making an **effigy** of the goddess especially for the festival. Each evening for nine days there is a special **arti** ceremony, followed by a meal and dancing.

At Dassehra ('the tenth day'), when Durga goes away, women kiss the effegy of the goddess goodbye. It is then lowered into the Ganges, where it sinks into the holy waters.

At Dassehra Hindus also celebrate how Prince Rama won a battle with the demon Ravana. Ravana had stolen his wife and taken her to his kingdom. Effigies of Ravana are burnt on bonfires and the battle is acted out in plays called *Ramleelas*. In Delhi, the capital of India, there is an enormous firework display.

These children are celebrating the festival of Holi

23

Other Hindu holy places

India is a huge country. There are hundreds of Hindu **holy** places spread across it. It can be difficult to reach many of them. People travel by planes, trains and buses, but there are many poor people who travel on carts or on foot. However, Hindus believe that the more effort they make on a **pilgrimage**, the more they improve their **karma** and move closer to **moksha**.

Some Hindus gather water from the River Ganges at Varanasi. Then they walk to the south of India to a famous **temple** at Rameshwar to offer the water to the god Shiva. This is a journey of 3840 kilometres (2400 miles)!

This is the festival of Rath Yatra in the town of Puri

Puri

Pilgrims travel to the east coast to Puri to worship Vishnu. At the Rath Yatra festival in June or July, an enormous chariot containing an **effigy** of Vishnu is dragged through the streets. Over 4000 worshippers help to pull it along.

Pilgrims try to show great respect at holy places. Many pilgrims will give up certain foods as a sign of respect to the gods.

In the north of India is an ancient pilgrimage site called Badrinath. Worshippers of the god Vishnu climb a mountain to reach it. The weather can make the climb so dangerous that the temple is only open for six months of the year. On the west coast of India at Dwarka, there is a mighty temple to Krishna, one of the best-loved gods.

Some pilgrims bring home beads or charms for good luck

Hindu family ceremonies

Hindu priests work out special dates by looking at the position of the stars and making charts called horoscopes. Priests draw up horoscopes for new-born babies, to tell what their lives will be like. This is done at the baby's naming ceremony, around 10 days after its birth.

Hindus take part in several other family ceremonies during their lifetime. These are called samskaras. One samskara is for boys about 8 years old. The boy sits with his father and a priest around a **sacred** fire. They say prayers, then the priest loops a thread of strong cotton around the boy's shoulder. This marks the beginning of adulthood. The boy is meant to wear the thread for the rest of his life.

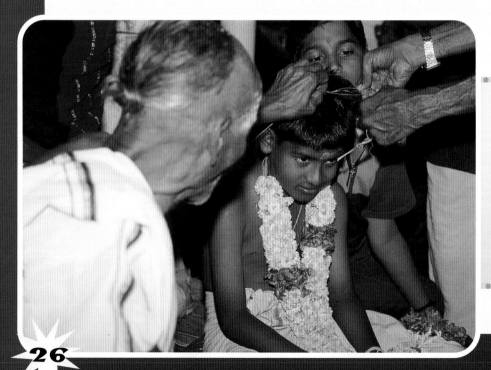

This Hindu boy is taking part in a sacred thread ceremony

A Hindu wedding can be a huge celebration, lasting for several days, with hundreds of people invited to the wedding feast. The bride and groom are often chosen for each other by their parents. A Hindu bride usually wears a dress called a sari and beautiful gold jewellery. They walk seven steps around a sacred fire, making a special promise to each other at each step. After the wedding, the bride goes to live with her husband's family.

This Hindu couple are getting married

Mahatma Gandhi – a Hindu holy man

In January 1997, an important ceremony was held on the banks of the Ganges at Allahabad. Thousands of people watched and prayed as the final **urn of ashes** of a great Hindu leader was scattered into the **holy** river. This leader was a man called Mahatma Gandhi.

Mahatma Gandhi was killed in 1948 by a man who disagreed with his teachings

Gandhi lived in India from 1869 to 1948 and grew up to be a lawyer. At that time, there was a lot of fighting in India between British soldiers, Hindus and **Muslims**. Gandhi felt strongly that no one should use violence to get what they wanted. Instead, he led thousands of people in peaceful protests such as **sit-ins** and **hunger strikes**. He encouraged Indians of different **religions** to be friends.

Gandhi also worked hard to help poor people. Most Hindus believe that everyone is born into a different class of importance in society. The lowest people are given the dirtiest jobs. Other Hindus won't have anything to do with them. Gandhi thought this was wrong. He showed great kindness to these 'untouchables' and worked hard to make their lives better. He called them Harijans, which means children of God.

This illustration from the Bhagavad Gita shows the god Krishna

Gandhi and the Bible

Gandhi found strength and bravery in reading a Hindu holy book called the Bhagavad Gita. Its hero is the god of love, Krishna, who teaches people to do their duty and think of others before themselves. Gandhi's other favourite book was a part of the **Christian** Bible called the New Testament. This tells about the life of Jesus, who taught that it was important to help poor people, just as Gandhi himself believed.

Glossary

arti   main ceremony of worship at a Hindu temple

Aryans   race of people who lived in India in ancient times

Buddhists   people who follow the teachings of the Buddha

chant   say something rhythmically over and over again

Christians   people who follow the spiritual teachings of a man called Jesus Christ, who lived around 2000 years ago

civilization   society of people who live together in an organized way, sharing laws and beliefs

dedicated   made important for just one person or thing

effigy   picture or model of a god

ghats   broad steps down to the edge of a holy river, where Hindu cremations often take place

glacier   slowly moving field of ice, found high up a mountain

holy (holiest)   blessed by God or belonging to God. (Holiest is the most holy.)

hunger strike   when people protest about something they disagree with by refusing to eat anything, making themselves ill

Jains   people who follow a religion that began over 2500 years ago. The founder, Mahavira, taught a respect for life and all living things.

karma   belief that the more good deeds you do in this life, the more you will be rewarded in the next life

lingam   specially shaped piece of stone – a symbol for the god Shiva

mantra short prayer or saying that a worshipper says over and over to help them concentrate on God

meditate to sit absolutely still and think very deeply on just one thing, trying to understand it better

moksha when a person's soul becomes free from living and dying and returns to Brahman

murti picture or statue of a god that is placed in a shrine

Muslim person who follows a religion called Islam, based on the teachings of a prophet called Muhammad (pbuh)

pilgrimage (**pilgrims**) journey someone makes to a holy place especially to worship there. (Pilgrims are the people who do this.)

puja offerings and worship Hindus make to a shrine

religion organized way of worshipping a God or gods

sacred something believed to be special to a God or gods

shrine place of worship that is special for a certain holy person or thing

Sikhism religion that began in India over 500 years ago, and grew from the teachings of a man called Guru Nanak

sit-in when people protest about something they disagree with by sitting down in an important place and refusing to move

soul part of a person that does not die when their body dies, sometimes called the spirit

symbol something that stands for something else

temple building where people worship a God or gods

urn of ashes when a person is cremated, the ashes of their burnt remains can be kept in a sealed jar called an urn

Index

Allahabad 18, 19, 28
arti ceremony 15, 22

Bible 29
Brahman 6, 9, 11, 12, 17, 20

cows, holy 7
cremations 11
cycle of death and rebirth 6, 11, 19

Diwali 23
Durga 12, 22–3

festivals 21, 22–3, 24, 25

Gandhi, Mahatma 28–9
Ganges 4, 5, 10, 11, 16, 18, 23,
    24, 28
Ganges legend 8–9
Gangotri 4, 18
gods and goddessess 8–9, 12–13,
    14, 15, 16–17, 21, 22–23, 25

Haridwar 15, 18
Hinduism 5, 6–7, 20
Holi 23
holy books 20–1, 22, 29
holy men 9, 14
holy places 10, 18, 19, 24–5
household shrines 13, 16–17

karma 18, 24
Krishna 25, 29
Kumbh Mela 19

mantras 17
moksha 6, 9, 11, 18, 19, 24
murtis 13, 15, 16, 17

naming ceremonies 26
Navaratri 22

pilgrimage 18–19, 24–25
priests 14, 15
puja 14, 16, 17

Ramayana 21
reincarnation 6

sacred thread ceremony 26
Shiva 9, 10, 12, 13, 17
Sikhism 5

temples 14–15, 21, 25

Upanishads 20, 21

Varanasi 10–11, 17, 19, 24
Vedas 20
Vishnu 12, 13, 21, 24

weddings 27
worship 14–17